·KINGFISHER·

SEE INSIDE

A GALLEON

SERIES EDITOR **R.J. UNSTEAD**

KINGFISHER BOOKS

Series Editor
R. J. Unstead

Author
Jonathan Rutland
Revised by Mary Connatty

Illustrators
John Berry, Michael Trim

Kingfisher Books, Grisewood & Dempsey Ltd,
Elsley House, 24–30 Great Titchfield Street,
London W1P 7AD
This second revised edition published in 1988 by Kingfisher Books
Copyright © Grisewood & Dempsey Ltd 1977, 1986, 1988

BRITISH LIBRARY CATALOGUING IN PUBLICATION DATA
Rutland, Jonathan
    See inside a galleon.—3rd ed.—
    (See inside)
    1. Galleons—History—Juvenile
    literature
    I. Title
    359.3′2   V767

ISBN 0-86272-327-2

Printed in Hong Kong

CONTENTS

War at Sea

For 2000 years, from the battle of Salamis in 480 BC in which a tiny Greek fleet destroyed the mighty navy of Persia, until the battle of Lepanto in 1571 in which a Christian fleet defeated the Turks, war at sea was fought mainly in long, oared ships called galleys. These were sleek, fast and very manoeuvrable. Warships often also carried sails, but these were lowered before action. At this time, sails were used mainly for merchant ships.

However, during the Middle Ages the rig of sailing ships was slowly improved. A new type of sail became common – the triangular lateen, or fore-and-aft, sail. This could be swung to catch the wind, making the ship much easier to control. Carracks and caravels – small ships with three or four masts and a combination of square and lateen sails – were developed. In such vessels, the great explorers sailed round Africa to India, and across the Atlantic to the West Indies.

Long-distance voyaging was soon followed by long-distance sea warfare. To meet this need, shipwrights of the 1500s developed the ships of explorers like Christopher Columbus into heavily-armoured ships built specially for battle. These were the 'great ships' or galleons, which were to dominate war at sea for the next 300 years.

On May 11, 1588, the huge Spanish Armada set sail from Lisbon. At the heart of the fleet were 22 Spanish and Portuguese galleons – among the biggest, most powerful warships of their day. But the great galleons were also heavy and slow to manoeuvre. Meanwhile in England, Sir Francis Drake and Sir John Hawkins had sparked a revolution in galleon design. Their fleet was made up of sleeker, more nimble ships with long-distance guns – a breakthrough in ship design that was to secure the defeat of the Spanish fleet and set the pattern for galleon design over the next 200 years.

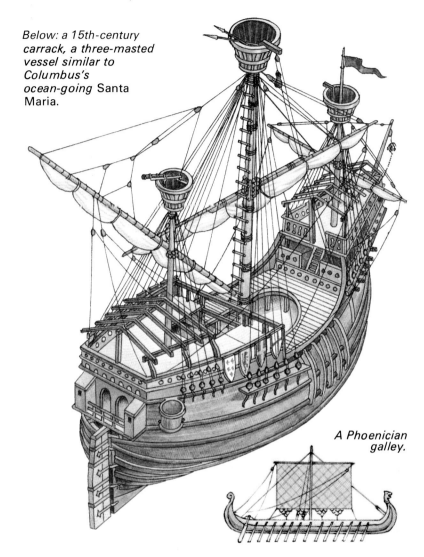

Below: a 15th-century carrack, a three-masted vessel similar to Columbus's ocean-going Santa Maria.

A Phoenician galley.

Below: The Ark Royal *was the flagship of Lord Howard of Effingham. It had 55 guns, and was built to John Hawkins' brand-new 'race' designs (see page 4).*

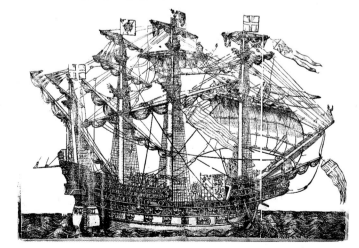

Opposite: The port of Lisbon was a bustling centre of commerce during the 15th century. The high decks and bulky design of the galleon in the picture was typical of the ships that sailed in the Armada.

Built for Battle

Like most 16th-century warships, the galleon in this picture has three masts – the mizzen mast (at the stern, or back of the ship), the mainmast (in the middle) and the foremast (at the front). The first galleons also had an extra mast at the stern, called the bonaventure mizzen.

As you can see, the fore and main masts have three square sails, while the mizzen has a square topsail and a triangular fore-and-aft sail. The two small sails at the bow are the spritsail (under the bowsprit) and the sprit topsail – these made the ship easier to steer. You can read more about sails and rigging on pages 12 and 13.

The galleon in the picture is a later version of the 'race-built' ship designed by John Hawkins for Queen Elizabeth I. On earlier warships, the raised decks, or castles, were much higher. The castles provided fighting platforms from which soldiers could fire down into enemy ships with small 'man-killing' guns. These high castles made the ships top-heavy, slow and difficult to control.

The big 'ship-killing' guns developed in the 16th century were too heavy to place high up on the castle, and in galleons they were mounted fairly low in the ship and were fired through gun-ports, or openings in the side of the ship. The Spanish galleons used in the great Armada had both high castles and heavy ship-killing guns, which had a short range.

To suit Francis Drake's new type of sea battle, Hawkins invented a new kind of fighting ship. His method was to cut down the high castles, lengthen the ship and fit it with heavy guns with a longer range. Because his ships were not top-heavy, they were easier to handle than the clumsy Spanish 'floating fortresses'. Hawkins' new designs were called 'race ships', not because they were fast but because their castles were cut down, or 'razed'.

The galleon is around 45 m (150 ft) long, and 12 m (40 ft) wide, and carries over 50 guns (you can see two rows of these in the picture).

The slender beakhead at the bow was probably copied from earlier galleys – in which it was used for ramming. On the galleon the beakhead carried the figurehead, and contained the crew's lavatories. The carved and gilded structure built on at the stern is the gallery.

Bowsprit

Foremast —

Mainmast

Mizzen mast

Poop

Quarter-deck

Half-deck

Below Decks

In the large cutaway picture below you can see inside the galleon. A few sailors slept in the forecastle (1), but most lived on the deck below, the gun deck (2). Here, although the cannons took up a lot of space, there was at least plenty of light and air (from the gunports, and from gratings and hatches in the deck above). The officers' 'cabins' were in the stern section of this deck (under the captain's cabin – 16). They consisted of little more than canvas screens which were moved before battle. One officer described his cabin as 'a thing much like to some gentleman's dog kennel'.

Often many of the crew had to sleep on the next deck down, the orlop (3). At or below the waterline, with no ports to let in light or air, this deck was dark and smelly. During battle the surgeon worked down here. The anchor cable locker (5), the cookhouse with its brick-lined fire (7), the cannonball store (9) and the sail locker (11) were also all on the orlop deck.

Below this was the hold (12) where barrels of water, beer, salt meat and other provisions were stored, alongside spare sails and ropes – and where younger members of the crew were sent for a punishment known as 'holding'. The offender was simply lowered into the hold for an hour or two of darkness, dampness and stench. The eerie light of a single lamp was often added to bring out the rats and cockroaches.

The very bottom of the hull, the bilge, was packed with stone ballast (6) which helped to stop the galleon heeling over dangerously. Other parts numbered are the capstans (10) and the bits, to which the anchor cable was secured (4).

Above: The richly carved and gilded stern of a French galleon. Such ornamental sterns were merely for show. They were very expensive, and could make a ship top-heavy and unstable.

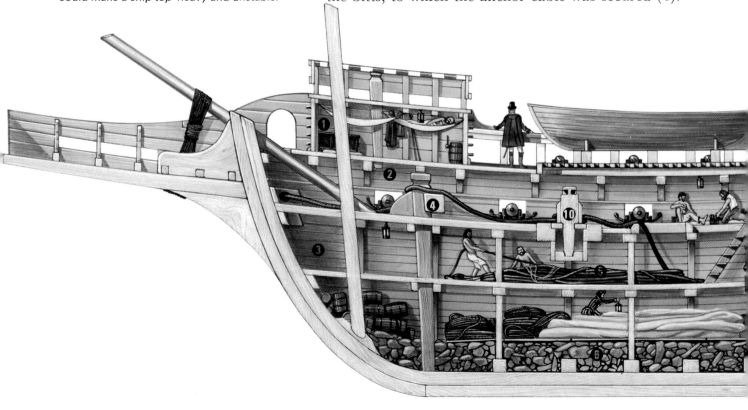

Left: A seaman of 400 years ago – there was no uniform. Most of the food and drink on board was stored in barrels like the one in the picture, so the cooper (the man who made and looked after the barrels) was an important man. Salt beef in a good barrel could be stored for many years – but soon went bad if the barrel was split or holed.

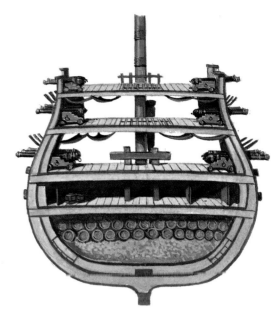

Below: A cutaway view of a two-decker galleon. The two decks referred to are those below the upper deck – the gun deck (2) and the orlop (3).

Above: A cross-section of a three-decker. You can see hammocks slung from the ceilings of the gun decks, and by the mast on the lower gun deck the bitts – heavy timbers to which the anchor cable was secured.

The galleon's pump (8) was used to draw any water that might have seeped into the bilges. The capstans (10) were used to haul heavy loads and to raise the anchors.

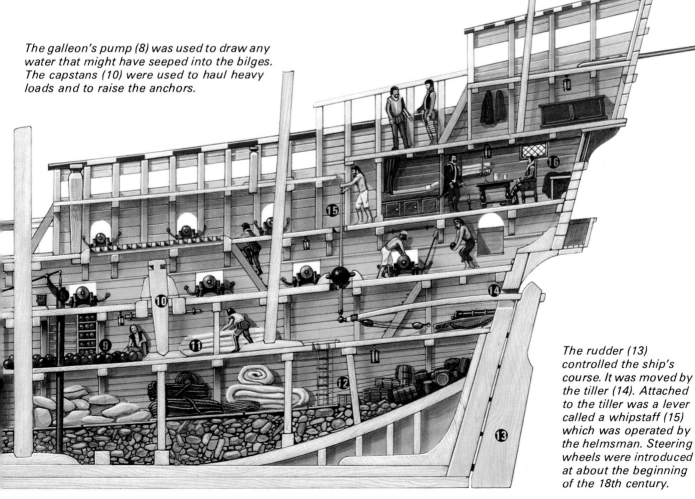

The rudder (13) controlled the ship's course. It was moved by the tiller (14). Attached to the tiller was a lever called a whipstaff (15) which was operated by the helmsman. Steering wheels were introduced at about the beginning of the 18th century.

7

Before Sailing

The quayside is busy with activity as food, drink, and equipment arrive for loading, while on board seamen check rigging, sails, guns and so on. You can see provisions being taken aboard through hatches in the galleon's side. Smaller barrels were usually rolled up a plank. Heavy items such as guns, or the largest barrels (which weighed nearly half a tonne) were lifted by a crane on the quay, or by ropes passing over pulleys on the yard, and lowered into the ship through hatches in the deck. But once on board there were no cranes to help, and even the half-tonne barrels had to be taken down to the hold and stowed by hand. The small cutaway section below shows men stowing provisions in the hold.

Below: In the foreground carpenters are working on the ship's boats, while other members of the crew check and move stores that have just been delivered.

A SEAMAN'S FOOD

The captain took on enough stores for the round trip – which could last several months. These might include around four tonnes of salt beef and two of salt pork; some salt fish, and about 10,000 kilograms of biscuits. There would also be dried peas, oatmeal, suet, butter (or oil, which kept better), cheese, and some casks of vinegar (this was used in cooking to hide the taste of stale or bad food, and it was used for cleaning the timbers). To drink there was around 54,000 litres (10,000 gallons) of beer, and less than half that amount of water!

Below: In the cutaway part at the stern you can see the admiral discussing the voyage with some of his captains.

Yo-heave-ho

The picture below shows a gang of men turning the capstan to raise the anchor. The anchor cable is far too thick to wind round the capstan. Instead an endless 'messenger rope' is used. At the hawsehole where the anchor cable enters the ship it is lashed (or nipped) on to the messenger rope by a length of thin rope called a nipper.

Turning the capstan winds in the messenger rope, which brings the anchor cable with it. As more anchor cable comes in through the hawsehole nippermen lash it to new stretches of the messenger rope. Then they undo the first nippers from the anchor cable which is aboard, and it is passed down through a hatch and coiled neatly in the hold.

Above: While the anchor is weighed, other members of the crew haul up the yards, and unfurl the sails.

Below: A fiddler plays a jaunty tune on his violin to help the sailors keep up a steady rhythm at the capstan. Sailors often worked to songs, or 'shanties'.

Weighing Anchor

An anchored ship does not float directly above its anchor. If it did, the anchor flukes (the spikes) would not dig into the sea-bed, and when the ship was lifted by the tide or a wave it would lift the anchor off the bottom.

So when the crew begin to wind in the anchor cable, it is not the anchor that moves but the entire galleon – shortening the cable pulls the ship through the water until it is above the anchor. Winding the cable in still more lifts the anchor off the sea-bed – the anchor is 'aweigh', and the galleon is free to move. As the anchor is lifted off the bottom and the wind fills the sails, the galleon is at last 'under way'.

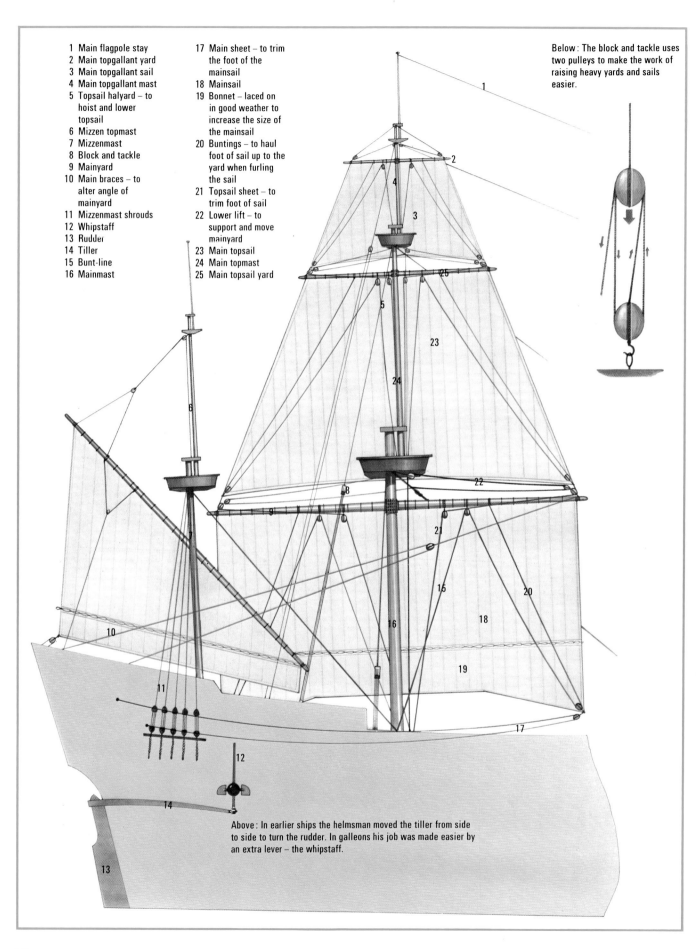

1 Main flagpole stay
2 Main topgallant yard
3 Main topgallant sail
4 Main topgallant mast
5 Topsail halyard – to
   hoist and lower
   topsail
6 Mizzen topmast
7 Mizzenmast
8 Block and tackle
9 Mainyard
10 Main braces – to
   alter angle of
   mainyard
11 Mizzenmast shrouds
12 Whipstaff
13 Rudder
14 Tiller
15 Bunt-line
16 Mainmast

17 Main sheet – to trim
   the foot of the
   mainsail
18 Mainsail
19 Bonnet – laced on
   in good weather to
   increase the size of
   the mainsail
20 Buntings – to haul
   foot of sail up to the
   yard when furling
   the sail
21 Topsail sheet – to
   trim foot of sail
22 Lower lift – to
   support and move
   mainyard
23 Main topsail
24 Main topmast
25 Main topsail yard

Below: The block and tackle uses two pulleys to make the work of raising heavy yards and sails easier.

Above: In earlier ships the helmsman moved the tiller from side to side to turn the rudder. In galleons his job was made easier by an extra lever – the whipstaff.

Masts, Sails and Rigging

The three *masts* are – from bow to stern – the foremast, mainmast and mizzen. The fore and main masts are both made of three *spars* (poles), called – from bottom to top – the mast, topmast and topgallant mast. The mizzen has no topgallant mast. The *sails* take their names from their mast: for example, on the foremast they are the foresail, the fore topsail, and the fore

topgallant sail. The *yards* – the poles from which the square sails hang – are named after their sail (main yard, main topsail yard and so on). The sloping spar at the bow is the bowsprit. The small sail at its end is the spritsail topsail, while the sail under the bowsprit is the spritsail.

RIGGING

The galleon's sails and spars were supported and controlled by a complicated mass of rigging. The sailors had to know the name and position of every rope. Their safety and the ship's depended on their being able to find the right one without a moment's delay – even in darkness.

There are two main types of rigging – 'standing' rigging, which is fixed and supports the masts; and 'running' rigging, which is used to raise or trim (adjust) the sails and yards. Standing rigging consists of shrouds, which run from the masthead to the ship's sides, and stays which run from the masthead to another mast or to some other part of the ship. Ratlines tied across each set of shrouds make rope ladders for the seamen to climb. Running rigging consists of 'sheets' (for trimming sails), 'halyards' (for raising or lowering yards and sails), and 'braces' (for setting the angle of a yard). You can see in the large picture some of the ropes, and how they work.

Above: A galleon sets sail. A gang of seamen unfurl the mainsail, and others in the main top adjust the running rigging.

Below: High winds could tear sails to shreds, so before a storm they had to be 'shortened'. In the picture the foresail is being furled.

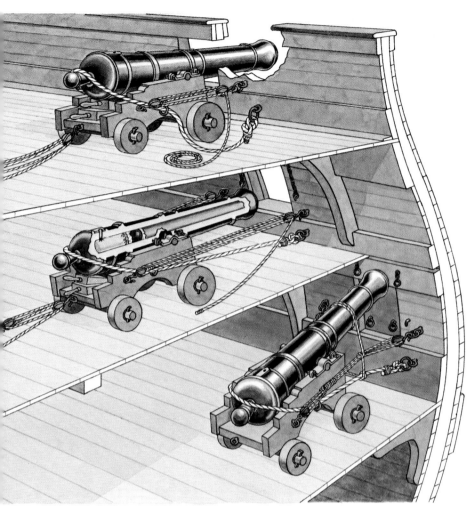

Left: Two main types of cannon were used in the battles of the Armada fought in the English Channel. One was cast in a single piece of bronze and loaded from the muzzle end. The other was made on the principle of a wooden barrel, with wrought-iron staves or strips and hoops welded together. It had a detachable powder chamber, or breech piece.

The top gun shown here is run out ready for firing, its muzzle sticking out through the open gun port. When the gun is fired the force of the explosion sending the shot forwards pushes the gun back – this is called the recoil. The middle gun is shown in the recoil position – the ropes stop it rolling too far. This gun is cut away to show the touch hole, cartridge, wadding and shot – these are described in the picture at the top of the facing page.

When not in action the gun was firmly tied down. The big guns weighed two or three tonnes, and if one broke loose in rough weather it could cause enormous damage to ship and crew.

TACTICS

During the 16th century, cannon fire was not very accurate and a huge amount of shot was wasted. Although the tactics used by the English during their battles against the Armada mainly involved keeping out of range of the Spanish guns and firing at long range, they could actually do more damage when fighting at close range – as they did during the Battle of Gravelines.

Battle at Sea

The galleons of the Spanish Armada were traditional 16th-century fighting ships. The raised decks fore and aft were like castles, and were manned by soldiers like castles on land. During battles, ships would come within close range of each other so that the soldiers could swing themselves onto the enemy's decks and fight hand-to-hand. The Spanish galleons also had gun decks with heavy cannons, but because of their high castles these ships were difficult to manoeuvre.

Francis Drake changed these fighting methods completely. He trained his sailors to handle the new 'race' ships expertly, and to man the new long-range guns with great skill. He created a new form of attack by sailing his ships into battle 'line ahead' of each other – that is, one after the other. In this way,

the English ships could fire lethal broadsides at the enemy while sailing past them.

On board, when the order was given to 'clear the decks', sailors hurried to clear the gundecks of hammocks, bedding, tables and so on. Others swarmed up the rigging to tie the yards securely. The boatswain and carpenter prepared their tools and materials to repair any damage to the hull or rigging. The surgeon laid out his instruments, ready to remove splinters, to bandage wounds and to amputate limbs. The gun crews set out their tools and shot, together with tubs of water to cool the overheated guns. They spread sand and salt on the deck to make it less slippery. Then they loaded their guns, opened the gun ports, and wheeled the guns out ready to fire.

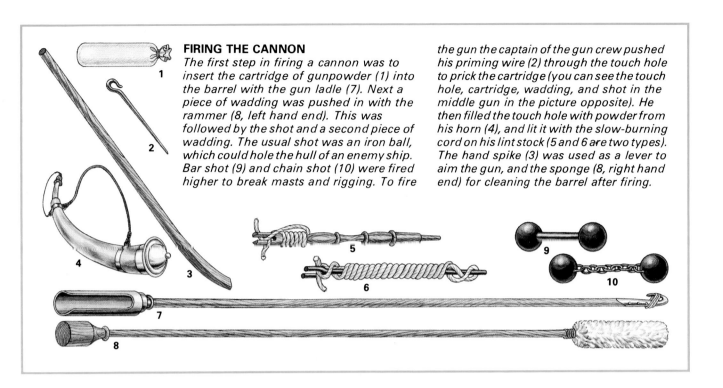

FIRING THE CANNON

The first step in firing a cannon was to insert the cartridge of gunpowder (1) into the barrel with the gun ladle (7). Next a piece of wadding was pushed in with the rammer (8, left hand end). This was followed by the shot and a second piece of wadding. The usual shot was an iron ball, which could hole the hull of an enemy ship. Bar shot (9) and chain shot (10) were fired higher to break masts and rigging. To fire the gun the captain of the gun crew pushed his priming wire (2) through the touch hole to prick the cartridge (you can see the touch hole, cartridge, wadding, and shot in the middle gun in the picture opposite). He then filled the touch hole with powder from his horn (4), and lit it with the slow-burning cord on his lint stock (5 and 6 are two types). The hand spike (3) was used as a lever to aim the gun, and the sponge (8, right hand end) for cleaning the barrel after firing.

Below: The gun deck during battle. Some men are busy at the guns, while others bring more shot. Smoke from the guns is blown back into the ship, and there is little light or air. The scene is crowded, and confused.

Life at Sea

Life on a galleon was hard and uncomfortable. The crew slept and ate on the gundecks. Gunports and hatches could be opened to let in light and air only in fine weather, so conditions were often dark, airless, smelly – and wet. The galleon's timbers 'worked' (moved), and in rough seas seams opened, letting in gushes of water.

Cockroaches, rats and a variety of bugs were common. The food was frequently rancid, too hard to chew, or full of weevils; the beer was sour; fresh fruit and vegetables were rare. During a long voyage far more seamen died of illness than in battle.

Right: It was too dangerous to light the cookhouse fires when the sea was rough, but during calm weather the cook could boil salt beef, pork or fish, and peas and dumplings.

Right: The crew slept in hammocks or on the floor, and ate at rough tables set up between the guns. In the picture the men at the table are enjoying a mug of chocolate – the most popular hot drink on board.

Pigs, goats, chickens or other animals were kept in pens on the galleon to provide fresh meat, eggs, butter, and cheese – mostly for the captain, and officers' tables. Sometimes the captain had his own cook, and a special oven in which food could be baked or roasted (in the main cookhouse the only way of cooking was by boiling).

JOBS AT SEA

In rough seas a sailor's work was difficult and dangerous. He had to climb up in the rigging to take in sails, or to fit new ones – a high wind could tear the canvas or break masts.

In fair weather the crew was kept busy swabbing the decks, manning the pumps, trimming the sails, cleaning and checking the guns, and doing repairs around the galleon.

Above: Sewing up any rips in the canvas sails, and checking the ropes for wear were just two of the many repair jobs which kept sailors busy at sea.

Right: Planks were curved by clamping them down into the right shape and then steaming them over a fire.

Right: Most of the timbers of a ship's frame are curved, like the ribs seen in the cutaway. You can also see diagonal supports inside the hull.

Frames (ribs)

Step for the mainmast

Diagonal struts

Designing a Galleon

Early shipwrights designed vessels mainly by eye. They watched any ships visiting their home port, compared their shapes, and saw how well they sailed. They developed an eye for a seaworthy vessel, and when building a ship followed a picture in their mind's eye.

But it was not practical to construct a large, complicated galleon in this way. By the late 1500s shipwrights usually drew detailed plans for the shipyard. From about 1650 they often made a scale model as well, like the one shown here.

Galleons were made of oak, a very strong and hard wood, and a single ship needed around 2000 trees. Its length was usually three or four times its greatest width. The underwater lines were based on fish shapes – rounded at the bow (like a cod's head) and narrowing down to a slim streamlined stern (like a mackerel's tail).

Above: Shipbuilders went to the forests armed with moulds of the ship's parts. They searched for trees to match the shapes.

Below: The amount of gold decoration on a galleon in the 1600s is clearly seen in the horseman on the beakhead. The wreaths around the gunports are also gilded.

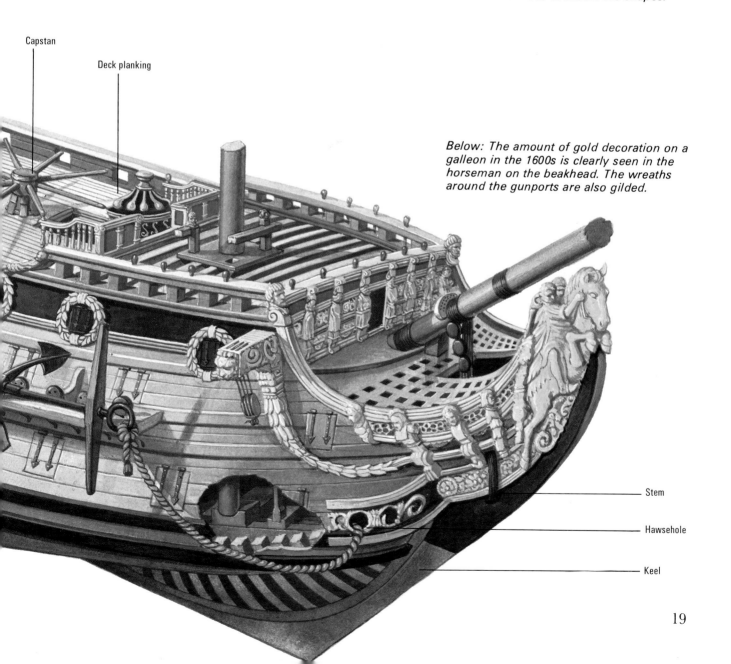

Capstan

Deck planking

Stem

Hawsehole

Keel

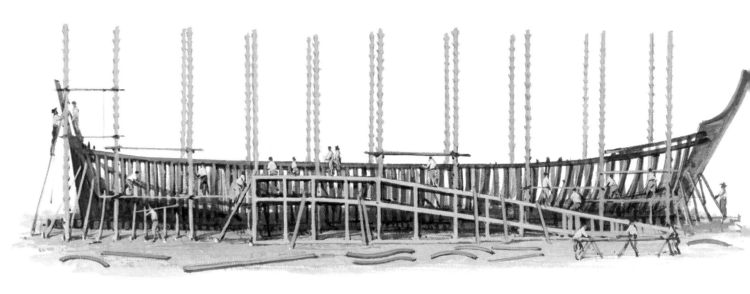

Building a Galleon

The first step was to lay the keel – the backbone on which the rest of the frame was built up. As this was often 30 metres (100 ft) or more long, it was made of several lengths of timber jointed and bolted together. The stempost and sternpost – which formed the bow and stern – were then jointed and bolted to the keel. The joint between sternpost and keel was strengthened with a massive timber 'knee', held in place with long bolts.

The V-shaped ground timbers on which the ribs would be built up were now bolted to the keel. To hold them firmly in place a keelson was added. This was an upper keel which slotted over the middle of each V piece and was bolted to the keel – thus clamping the ground timbers between keel and keelson. Next the ribs were built up on their ground timbers. Like the keel they were too large to be shaped from a single log, and were made of several pieces joined together. You can see the basic skeleton of keel, sternpost, stempost and ribs in the picture above.

Left: Sawing planks. Below: The carpenter's tools.

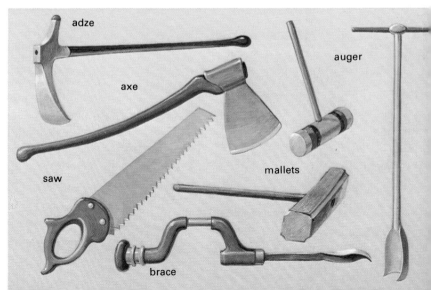

adze

axe

auger

saw

mallets

brace

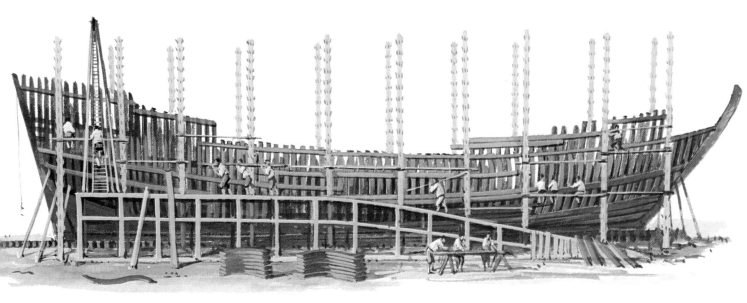

Above: On the level of each deck, beams were fixed across the ship from the rib on one side to its partner on the other. The joint between rib and beam was strengthened with 'knees' (you can see piles of these on the ground in the picture).

The strength of the ship depended on its skeleton, so all joints had to be really firm – and all the timbers really massive (they were often over ½ metre – 1½ ft – square). Once the skeleton was complete, planking could begin. The planks, up to 13 cm (5 in) thick, were laid edge to edge, and were held in place with wooden pegs called treenails – iron nails would soon rust away. The hull then had to be made watertight by caulking before it was ready for launching.

Above: Caulking or waterproofing was done by forcing yarn or tar between the planks of the hull. After this, the underwater planks might be coated with tar and hair, and sheathed with thin planks to protect the hull from barnacles and worms. To launch the galleon (below), workmen first built a 'cradle' under the keel, and fixed supports between the hull and cradle to hold the ship upright (you can see these supports near bow and stern in the picture). Next the scaffolding, the supporting poles, and the blocks on which the keel had been laid (and which had taken the vessel's weight until now) were removed. Finally gangs of men on shore and at capstans on barges in the water hauled and pushed the cradle and its load down into the water. The cradle slid along a specially prepared launching way – a shallow trough well greased with tallow (animal fat). The lighter the hull, the easier it was to launch, so the final 'fitting out' was done after launching. Masts, spars, and so on were added when the hull was afloat.

Finding the Way

Francis Drake sailed his galleon *Golden Hind* around the world, and many other captains made long voyages across uncharted oceans. They found their way partly by guesswork, partly by following steady 'trade winds', and partly by using the sun and stars.

On setting sail from port the captain knew his direction from his compass, and could estimate his speed. So after a few hours (timed with a sand glass) he could mark his new position on a chart. This was called 'dead reckoning'. It depended on the captain's skill in estimating how far the wind and current had taken him off course.

The log line helped to measure speed. A length of cord was knotted at equal spaces, and a piece of wood fixed to one end was dropped overboard. The number of knots slipping through a seaman's fingers in one minute gave the approximate speed in 'knots' (nautical miles an hour).

On the equator the sun is overhead at noon. The farther north or south one travels, the lower the sun is in the sky. So by measuring the sun's altitude at noon (its height above the horizon), sailors could work out their distance north or south of the equator (latitude).

Above: An early mariner's compass. The card and its magnetized needle pivoted on a pin.

Below: A map of the world drawn in 1570. Maps and charts helped the captain plot his course across the open seas.

Above: Using a backstaff to measure the sun's height above the horizon.

Below: Speed was checked by sand glass (left) and log line.

THE STORY OF THE ARMADA

In May 1588, Philip II of Spain sent his Great Armada, or armed fleet, to invade Britain. There were many different reasons behind this declaration of war. At one time, Spain had hoped for a long-lasting alliance. Henry VIII of England had married Catherine of Aragon in 1509, but the marriage was dissolved by Henry when Catherine failed to give him a male heir. This was deeply offensive to Catholic Spain, especially as Henry had gone against the decision of the Pope in divorcing Catherine. Relations between the two countries became more and more bitter, and when Queen Elizabeth I of England ordered that her Catholic cousin Mary, Queen of Scots should be beheaded in 1587, Philip took the opportunity of revenging her death by declaring war.

Philip had been gathering his great fleet together since the early 1580s. In 1580 he added Portugal to his empire and took over her navy, which included the finest fighting ships in the world. He also hired ships from Genoa, Venice, Ragusa, Naples and the Sicilian ports. The ships of the Great Armada included galleasses, huge vessels with both sails and oars; great cumbersome urcas, the freight carries of the Mediterranean; and the small manoeuvrable patches and pinnaces, which were to be used as messengers or for look-out duty. But of all the ships of King Philip's navy, the most important were the 22 Spanish and Portuguese galleons. These were the battleships – the protectors of the fleet and the vessels of attack.

Above: Sir Francis Drake, whose methods of sea warfare helped to revolutionize galleon design. The Spaniards called this famous sea adventurer 'El Draco' – The Dragon.

Left: Spanish galleons at the time of the Armada were huge, cumbersome and slow – 'floating fortresses' more suited to defence than attack.

Philip's plan was not to wage a war at sea against the English, but to carry soldiers to fight on English soil. To be successful he needed the help of the Duke of Parma, his greatest military captain, who had troops in the Netherlands. His idea was to sail the Armada up the Channel, link up with Parma's troops at Dunkirk and sail together to England.

On July 29, 1588 Captain Thomas Flemyng sailed into Plymouth Sound to report to Sir Francis Drake that he had sighted the Armada off the Lizard. He found Drake playing a game of bowls on Plymouth Hoe. His legendary reply to Flemyng's news – 'We have time to finish the game and beat the Spaniards' – was not just a matter of bravado. He knew the tides of Plymouth like the back of his hand, and was fully aware that it would be

another eight hours before he could move his fleet out of the harbour.

Later on that same evening, at high tide, Francis Drake and Lord Howard of Effingham, the English Commander-in-Chief, sailed their fleet of 54 ships out of Plymouth Sound. On the afternoon of the following day, the two fleets sighted each other through driving rain. It was difficult to see exactly how many ships made up the Spanish fleet, but one English observer said of the Armada that the sea 'groaned under the weight of ships'.

The English seamen were impressed by the way the Spanish kept in strict formation. Their fleet was spread out in a great arc, like the wings of a bird. In the 'body' were the slow-moving urcas, or transport ships. The Spanish Commander-in-Chief, the Duke of Medina, led the way in his flagship – a Portuguese galleon called the *San Martin*. With him were a group of Portuguese galleons and four galleasses, and galleons were also positioned on the wings and astern to protect the main body of the fleet.

The *San Martin de Portugal* was the flagship of the Spanish Commander-in-Chief – the Duke of Medina Sidonia. It was a huge 1000-ton galleon carrying 48 guns, and one of the proudest ships in the Portuguese navy (which had been taken by Philip II in 1580). It must have been immensely strong, because it suffered intense pounding by the English guns at the Battle of Gravelines and yet managed to get back to Spain after a horrific journey of nearly 3000 miles.

Above: In the first skirmish of the battle between the Spanish and English fleets, Lord Howard of Effingham, the Commander-in-Chief of the English Navy, attacked the leading flagship of the Armada in his own flagship – the Ark Royal.

It must have been very difficult for the Spanish fleet to keep in formation. The arc spread across more than six kilometres of sea, and all vessels were forced to keep pace with the slow, heavily-laden urcas. The great galleons had to shorten their sails to reduce their speed.

THE FIRST BATTLE

The signal to begin the battle came on the morning of July 31, when the Duke of Medina raised the standard of Spain on the main topmast of the *San Martin*. Lord Howard sent the pinnace *Disdain* to accept the challenge. The *Disdain* unloaded a single shot at the Spanish fleet. Howard then proceeded to fight the *San Martin* from his own flagship, the *Ark Royal*, while Drake took on the Spanish vice-flagship. The battle had all the air of a fight between medieval knights. Only a few shots were fired, and little damage was done. The English, in their new 'race-built' ships (see page 4), had no intention of coming within close range of the Spanish guns.

By accident, two great Spanish galleons were put out of action. The *Nuestra Senora del Rosario* collided with other ships and drifted astern of the fleet. She was captured by Drake and towed into Torbay where her captain and crew were taken prisoner. The *San Salvador* blew up, causing the death of many seamen, and was towed into Weymouth. A huge stock of her cannon balls and gunpowder was transferred to the English fleet.

The Armada carried on up the English Channel with the English fleet in pursuit. The next encounter took place off Portland Bill near Weymouth on August 2. A great deal of gunshot was wasted with very little damage done. The Spanish were frustrated that the English ships continued to keep out of the way of their powerful guns.

Two days later, the Armada reached the coast of the Isle of Wight. However, the English were determined to prevent the Spanish fleet from sheltering in the Solent which was the last safe anchorage point until the Thames.

During the third battle there was no wind to stir the sails of the mighty Spanish galleons, and it became the turn of the oared galleasses to take the brunt of the fight. Four great vessels were rowed into battle, with a huge galleon in tow to give extra fire-power. On the English side, Lord Howard of Effingham's race-built ships were towed into the fray by rowing boat.

For hours, the great ships pounded each other but again the damage done to either side was not great. Medina, when writing to Parma for more shot and supplies, complained that the English were unwilling to fight. He plainly failed to understand that Drake's method of fighting was not the traditional one of grappling the enemy ship and boarding it for battle, but firing broadsides at long range.

FIRESHIPS BY NIGHT

As the wind rose, the Spanish sails billowed into action once again, but they were unable to stop the nimble English fleet from making its escape.

Below: This engraving, commissioned by Lord Howard of Effingham, shows the engagement between Spanish and English fleets off the Isle of Wight.

The Armada continued on its journey towards Dunkirk on the Flemish shore. It was while sailing that the Duke of Medina learnt of a serious fault in the battle plans.

Large fighting ships such as galleons and galleasses need a deep water port for anchorage. While planning the 'Great Enterprise', Philip II had overlooked the fact that Dunkirk had only a shallow creek to offer the huge Spanish fleet. To make matters worse, the Duke of Parma failed to appear with either troops or fresh supplies. Greatly worried by the course of events, Medina was forced to anchor about eleven kilometres off Calais.

The English fleet instantly recognized its advantage. At anchor, the Armada was an obvious target for fireships. With the added help of Lord Seymour's Dover squadron, which now joined Howard and Drake, they began to fill eight old ships with explosives and waited for a favourable wind and tide.

Meanwhile, the Spanish ships were in trouble. The rising tide and winds caused their anchors to drag, and many ships became entangled. They prepared themselves for the English attack as best they could. Pinnaces were fitted with long grapnels, to tow the fireships away, and each ship was

Above: Blazing with fire and explosives, the eight fireships of the English Navy bore down upon the Armada as it lay harboured off Calais.

ordered to attach its anchor to a buoy. If a fireship came too close, the ship could cut its cable and make a quick retreat, leaving the anchor tied to the buoy. When the danger was past, the ships could return once again to rescue the anchors.

It was after midnight when the Spaniards first saw the glowing English fireships drifting towards them on the tide. Laden with gunpowder and shot, which exploded in all directions, they made a terrifying sight in the darkness. The Spanish panicked, cut their cables and collided with each other in their hurry to escape. Dragged by the strong currents, they narrowly escaped being wrecked off the Flemish shore.

BATTLE AT GRAVELINES

As day broke on August 8, Medina sighted the English fleet bearing down on his scattered fleet about eleven kilometres from Gravelines. With only four great galleons, he decided to stay and fight until his fleet could gather around him.

Francis Drake led the English attack in the *Revenge*. The Spanish ships were pounded by shot as his squadron opened fire at ninety metres range. Apalling damage was done to the Spanish hulls, and sails and castles were ripped and shattered by the English guns. The huge Portuguese galleon *San Felipe* was cut off and surrounded by some seventeen English ships, which pulverized her with gunshot.

Three great Spanish ships sank that day, and many others were badly damaged. The decks ran with the blood of the six hundred Spaniards that had been killed and the eight hundred wounded. Towards the evening, wind and driving rain brought the terrible battle of Gravelines to an end. Defeated and exhausted, the Spanish sailors struggled against the wind to keep their ships away from the deadly sandbanks of the Flemish coast.

As dawn broke the following day, the Spaniards waited for the final attack with heavy hearts, battered

ships and no ammunition. However, the English were also nearly out of ammunition, and so kept a cautious distance from the perilous sandbanks. Then, as they looked on, a remarkable thing happened. The wind suddenly changed direction, blowing the Armada away from the shore and into the North Sea. The Duke of Medina wrote, 'By God's mercy, we were saved by the wind'.

Pursued by the English fleet as far as the Firth of Forth, the Armada sailed north. It was in no condition to fight again, and Medina planned to save the remaining ships by carrying out repairs at sea while following the long route home – around the east coast of Britain, around the north of Scotland and back down the Atlantic Ocean. However, these rough seas were unknown to the Spanish sailors. Horrific Atlantic gales scattered the ships and wrecked many of them off the coasts of Scotland and Ireland. Of the 130 stately ships which had sailed so proudly from Lisbon, just over sixty limped home to the ports of northern Spain. Thousands more sailors died on that dreadful journey, and few of those who returned home were to survive the appalling hardships they had endured.

Overleaf: In this beautiful painting of an engagement between the Spanish and English fleets, the great galleons and galleasses of the Armada fly the red and gold flag of Spain. The English Navy fly the white and red flag of St George, while striped flags indicated different squadrons.

The English galleons chased the defeated Armada as far north as the Firth of Forth, but then gave up the chase as they had no gunpowder left. At the mercy of the Atlantic's storms, many Spanish galleons foundered on the rocky Scottish and Irish coasts. Among them was the Girona, whose golden treasure was discovered at the bottom of the sea near the Giant's Causeway in 1967.

GLOSSARY OF TERMS

Abaft Behind, towards the stern.

Abeam Across the ship, at right angles to its length.

Aft At or near the stern of a ship.

Ahead Directly in front of the bows.

Amidships In the middle of a ship.

Anchor Heavy piece of iron which digs into the sea bed to hold a ship to the spot.

Astern Backwards – behind the stern.

Athwartships Across the ship, from one side to the other.

Awash Level with the surface of the sea.

Ballast Heavy material such as stones in the bottom of the hold to help keep the ship upright.

Beak A strong projection of the prow (or bow) which smashed oncoming waves when a ship pitched or dipped low in a rough sea.

Beam Width of ship at its widest point.

Berth Place where a ship ties up.

Bilge The bottom of a ship.

Bonaventure An extra mizzen mast on a four-mast ship.

Boom A pole along the foot of a sail.

Bow The sharp front end of a ship.

Bowsprit A long spar at the bow.

Bridge Raised deck from which a ship is navigated.

Broadside Shots from all the guns on one side of a ship.

Bulkhead Wall dividing up the inside of a ship.

Buoy A floating marker moored in the water to guide or warn ships.

Buoyancy The ability of an object to float.

Capstan A revolving windlass or drum-shaped device for winding in anchor cable.

Carvel-built (Of a wooden ship): having its planks laid edge to edge.

Caulking Making seams between planks watertight with pitch (tar).

Chart Map of the sea and coastal waters.

Clinker-built (Of a wooden ship): having its planks overlapping.

Deck Nautical word for floor.

Dock The working area of a harbour where ships are loaded, unloaded and repaired.

Draught Depth of a ship below the water.

Fathom Unit of length used for measuring the depth of water, equal to 1.83 m (6 ft).

Following wind One blowing from astern (behind).

Forecastle, or Fo'c'sle Raised deck in the bows. Often used to describe accommodation in the bows for the crew.

Forward Near the front or bows.

Freeboard Height from waterline to the top of the hull.

Galley A ship's kitchen.

Gear Nautical word for machinery or equipment – e.g. steering gear, ship's gear (derricks, cranes etc. for loading cargo).

Gunwale (gunnel) Upper edge of a ship's or boat's side.

Hatch An opening in a deck, or its wooden cover.

Heel When a sailing ship is blown over to one side it is said to heel over.

Helm Steering control of a ship.

Hogging The tendency of a ship to droop at bow and stern when it rides over a wave.

Hold The lowest part of the hull, where cargo is stored.

Hull The body of a ship.

Keel The main timber at the bottom of a ship (the spine).

Knot A speed of a nautical mile an hour.

Lateen A triangular sail which is set along the ship ('fore-and-aft'), not across it.

Latitude Distance north or south of the equator, measured in degrees, from 0° on the equator to 90° at the poles.

Leeward Direction towards which the wind blows. The lee side of a ship is therefore the sheltered side, away from the wind.

Longitude Distance east or west of the Greenwich zero meridian, measured in degrees east or west of Greenwich.

Mizzen Fore-and-aft sail on after-most mast of a three-mast ship; also the mizzen may refer to the mast itself.

Right: An illustration from a book printed in 1585 shows fire bombs and cannon balls headed for a Swedish ship. Other kinds of shot commonly used were explosive bombs (hollow iron balls filled with gunpowder); hot shot (solid balls which were heated before being placed in the gun) and chain shot (two iron balls linked by a chain).

Moor To secure a ship, either against a quay, or by tying it to a mooring buoy, or by dropping anchor.

Nautical mile A distance of 1852 m (6076.1 ft).

Orlop A deck beneath the lower gundeck and above the hold.

Pitching The plunging and rising movements of a ship as it rides across the waves.

Poop The aftercastle: a raised deck at the stern.

Port The left-hand side of a ship, looking forward.

Porthole An opening in the side of a ship to let in light and air and for cannon to fire through.

Quarterdeck Part of upper-deck between stern and mizzen-mast.

Rake The slope of masts, funnels, bows, etc.

Ratlines Ropes knotted across the shrouds to provide a rope ladder to the masthead.

Rigging The ropes used to support masts, and to control sails and spars.

Rudder Large, flat wooden blade at the stern, used to turn a ship.

Sheet Rope used for setting and trimming a sail.

Shroud Rope from masthead to ship's side, supporting mast.

Spar Wooden pole such as mast or yard.

Spritsail A small square sail fitted to the bowsprit.

Square sail A sail set across the ship, from side to side.

Starboard Right hand side of ship.

Stay Rope which helps support a mast.

Stempost The curved timber at the bow to which a ship's sides are joined.

Stern The back of the ship.

Superstructure Upper parts of a ship, built on top of the hull.

Tiller Length of wood fitted to the top of the rudder, for steering.

Trim To adjust the balance of a ship or boat; to move yards or sails to suit wind. Also the way a ship floats in the water.

Wake or Wash The waves and foam caused by a moving ship.

Watch A spell of duty for a seaman.

Windward Direction from which the wind blows. The windward side is therefore the one exposed to the wind.

Yard A spar (or pole) slung across a mast to support a sail.

PHOTOGRAPHIC ACKNOWLEDGEMENTS

The publishers wish to thank the following for supplying photographs for this book: Page 1 Huntington Library, San Marino, California; 2 Giraudon; 3 British Museum, London; 22 Science Museum, London *top;* Michael Holford *bottom;* 23 National Portrait Gallery, London *top;* Peter Newark's Historical Pictures *bottom;* 24 Peter Newark's Western Americana *top;* Huntington Library, San Marino, California *bottom;* 25 Peter Newark's Western Americana; 27 Ulster Museum, Belfast; 28–29 Michael Holford.

INDEX

Inside front cover: On May 11, 1588 the great Spanish Armada set sail from Lisbon. On board were 30,000 soldiers as well as priests, doctors and legal administrators, ready to conquer and govern England. Yet instead of winning a glorious victory, the Armada suffered a humiliating defeat. In late September and October, about half the scattered fleet limped into the ports of Northern Spain. War-torn, battered by the sea and mostly beyond repair, they made a tragic contrast with the magnificent fleet which had set out four months before.

Inside back cover: The battles between the Armada and the English fleet took place in the English Channel between July 31 and August 8, 1588. The Spanish plan was to destroy the English fleet, link up with the Duke of Parma's troops at Dunkirk and sail across the Channel to invade England. However, the English fleet were not destroyed, the Duke of Parma failed to appear, and the defeated Armada was forced to retreat and make the long and disastrous journey home by sailing round the north of Scotland and down the Atlantic.